TULSA CITY-COUNTY LIBRARY

★ THE SHOCKING SECRET OF THE ELECTRIC EEL ★ . . . AND MORE!

BY ANA MARÍA RODRÍGUEZ

Enslow Publishing
101 W. 23rd Street
Suite 240
New York, NY 10011
USA
enslow.com

Acknowledgments
The author expresses her immense gratitude to all the scientists who
have contributed to the Animal Secrets Revealed! series. Their comments and
photos have been invaluable to the creation of these books.

Published in 2018 by Enslow Publishing, LLC.
101 W. 23rd Street, Suite 240, New York, NY 10011

Library of Congress Cataloging-in-Publication Data
Names: Rodriguez, Ana Maria, 1958- author.
Title: The shocking secret of the electric eel... and more! / Ana María
  Rodríguez.
Description: New York : Enslow Publishing, 2018. | Series: Animal secrets
  revealed! | Includes bibliographical references and index. | Audience:
  Grades 3 to 6.
Identifiers: LCCN 2017009698| ISBN 9780766087262 (library bound) | ISBN
  9780766088511 (pbk.) | ISBN 9780766088450 (6 pack)
Subjects: LCSH: Fishes—Behavior—Juvenile literature. | Animal
  defenses—Research—Juvenile literature.
Classification: LCC QL639.3 .R63 2017 | DDC 597.14/7—dc23
LC record available at https://lccn.loc.gov/2017009698

To Our Readers: We have done our best to make sure all websites in this book were
active and appropriate when we went to press. However, the author and the publisher have
no control over and assume no liability for the material available on those websites or on
any websites they may link to. Any comments or suggestions can be sent by email to
customerservice@enslow.com.

Photo Credits: Cover Bigone/Shutterstock.com; pp. 3 (top left), 6 © Yourthstock/
Dreamstime.com; pp. 3 (top right), 12, 15 Alexandra Grutter; pp. 3 (center left), 18, 22
Ryan Kaldari; pp. 3 (bottom right), 26, 27, 28 Courtesy of Jens De Meyer, Evolutionary
Morphology of Vertebrates, Ghent University, Belgium; pp. 3 (bottom left), 33, 35 Margaret
Marchaterre; p. 8 © Wrangel/Dreamstime.com.

★ CONTENTS ★

1
The Shocking Secret of the Electric Eel
Page 5

2
Parrotfish Don't Let the
Sea Bugs Bite
Page 11

3
The Secret of the Hairy-Legged
Jumping Spider
Page 17

4
Eels Let Food Get to Their Heads
Page 24

5
The Secret of the Underwater
Night Hummers
Page 31

Hands-on Activity . . . Page 40

Chapter Notes . . . Page 43

Glossary . . . Page 46

Further Reading . . . Page 47

Index . . . Page 48

ENTER THE WORLD OF ANIMAL SECRETS

In this volume of Animal Secrets Revealed!, you will tag along with scientists in the field or in the lab and discover intriguing adaptations that help animals survive in their environments. You will start your adventure in the United States, witnessing the leap-and-shock attack of the impressive electric eel. Next, you will dive at Australian coral reefs with parrotfish and discover how a cocoon of mucus lets them have a good night's sleep. In your next adventure, you will return to the United States and meet jumping spiders that can hear you come across the room, with their legs. Your next journey will take you to Belgium, where scientists discovered how the European eel can have two different head sizes. Finally, your journey will end on North America's West Coast, the land of fish that only sing at night.

Welcome to the world of animal secrets!

1
THE SHOCKING SECRET OF THE ELECTRIC EEL

Kenneth Catania is standing by the electric eels' aquarium, holding a net in his hand. He will use the net, which has a metallic rim and handle, to transfer eels from one tank to another. As he submerges the net in the water, some of the eels swim away from it, but others zoom toward it. In an instant, an eel leaps up and climbs along the net's rim and handle, firing a racket of high-voltage pulses. Then, the eel drops back into the water.[1] Catania is not hurt by the electric shocks; he is wearing insulating gloves that do not conduct electricity.

"This behavior was both literally and figuratively shocking," Catania said. "Under no other circumstances were eels observed to leap out of the water."[2]

Intrigued by the unexpected leap-and-shock behavior, Catania decided to study it. When he searched the scientific literature, he found a story from the early 1800s in South America. In the story, explorer Alexander von Humboldt wrote of eels attacking a group of horses that had stepped into a pool where the eels lived.

Electric eels can sense their surroundings by releasing low-voltage electric pulses.

"The eels emerged from the mud, swam to the surface, and attacked by pressing themselves against the horses while discharging," Catania said.[3]

The story became famous, but not everybody believed it. "The aggressive behavior of the eels, taking the offensive against the horses, seems the most fantastic and questionable part of the story," Catania said.

But now Catania had observed the "fantastic" behavior himself. He wondered, why would electric eels do this?

Sense, Twitch, Shock

Among fish that produce electricity, the eel is the most powerful. Most of its body is made of electrocytes, musclelike cells that produce electricity. All the electrocytes combined can discharge up to 600 volts.[4] This is five times the discharge of one electric socket in US households.

Before he investigated the eel's leap-and-shock behavior, Catania had studied how an eel's electric shocks affect prey. He found out that eels release three different types of electric pulses: low-voltage pulses for sensing, high-voltage pulses in pairs or triplets to make prey twitch, and a stream of high-voltage pulses to paralyze prey.[5] Sometimes, eels produce low-voltage pulses that help them sense other creatures in their environment. Other times, when they are hunting, eels combine the two types of high-voltage electric shocks.

Electric eels release high-voltage electric pulses to reveal the location of hidden prey.

Fish may hide and remain quiet, trying to escape the eel's attack. To make fish reveal their location, eels release two to three high-voltage pulses, several times. When shocked by these pulses, fish twitch. This creates vibrations in the water that eels can sense. Once it knows where the fish is, the eel produces a stream of high-voltage pulses that shock and paralyze the fish for a fraction of a second. In this instant, the eel captures the fish by sucking it into its mouth in a flash.[6]

Eels can also catch fish that swim by them. As soon as it feels the water movement, revealing a nearby fish, the eel discharges the stream of high-voltage pulses that paralyze the fish just enough for the eel to gobble it up.

It seemed to Catania that eels had another form of attack, leap-and-shock style. He had to design experiments to test his theory.

> **Science Tongue Twister**
> **The electric eel's scientific name is *Electrophorus electricus.***

Offense Is the Best Defense

Catania thought that the leap-and-shock behavior seemed to be a defense strategy that eels might use against a threat lurking outside the water. To study whether this was the case, Catania designed experiments to reveal the path electricity would follow when eels jumped and attacked

He used a plastic crocodile head to simulate a predator. To see the path electricity would take as the eel attacked the crocodile head, Catania dotted the plastic head with little lights. If the eel shocked the crocodile when it touched it with its snout, the areas would light up.

Catania held the crocodile prop with a gloved hand and approached the water in a tank with an eel in it. The eel rushed to the surface, raised above the water, and touched the crocodile head with its snout. As the eel climbed, the prop lit up! Catania repeated the experiment using a fake human arm covered with little lights. The result was the same. As the eel climbed on the arm above the water, the lights on the arm lit up.[7]

From these experiments, Catania also learned that the electric shock increased as the eels climbed higher. When eels attack this way, animals receive high-voltage shocks that cause them pain. The attack might also disable them.

The mysterious eel attack on horses, as described by Humboldt more than two hundred years ago, is not a myth. Eels can leap and shock large animals that approach them from outside the water. The painful electric shock is an effective way to encourage any animal to leave the eel's pond immediately. It would also discourage it from coming back.

2
PARROTFISH DON'T LET THE SEA BUGS BITE

Late at night, marine biologist Jennifer Rumney is walking quietly in a dark room. She won't turn the lights on. That might wake up the fish and ruin the experiment. Rumney studies parrotfish that she collects on Lizard Island Great Barrier Reef in Australia. These fish are well known for sleeping at night inside a cocoon made of mucus. Some scientists have proposed that the cocoon might protect parrotfish from predators, such as moray eels, that are trying to eat them. However, other scientists are not convinced.

Rumney is studying parrotfish in the lab of Dr. Alexandra Grutter at the University

A female parrotfish sleeps inside a mucus cocoon. To see the transparent cocoon, the scientists sprinkled sand on top.

Queensland. Grutter, Rumney, and their colleagues had another idea about what the purpose of the mucus cocoon might be.[1]

Bug-Cleaning Crew

In the waters of the Lizard Island coral reefs, small blood-sucking parasites called gnathiid isopods prey on parrotfish.

To solve this problem, parrot-fish have relied on another fish, appropriately called the cleaner fish. During the day, cleaner fish remove the parasites from the parrotfish's skin and eat them.

<table>
<tr><td>**Symbiosis**
Symbiosis is a relationship between two different organisms that provides benefits to both.</td></tr>
</table>

This symbiosis benefits both the cleaner fish, which get an easy meal, and parrotfish, which are rid of the parasites.[2]

At night, however, when parrotfish sleep, cleaner fish go off duty, but the blood-sucking parasites do not.

"I thought parrotfish might have other ways to avoid being infected by the isopods at night," Grutter said. "Sleeping inside a cocoon of mucus looked like a way to avoid isopod bites, just like a mosquito net would protect us from bugs while we sleep."[3]

Rumney decided to test the idea.

Don't Wake the Fish!

To test whether the mucus cocoons would protect parrotfish from the bites of gnathiid isopods, Rumney placed parrotfish in individual containers in the lab. At night, she turned the lab lights off and waited for the fish to make their cocoons and fall asleep.

Each night, parrotfish make the mucus in an organ near their gills. The mucus exits through the gills and, in about an hour, surrounds the body of the fish. The next morning, the

13

fish exit the mucus envelope and go about their daily activities. When night comes again and they go to sleep, parrotfish make another cocoon.

Rumney entered the room a few hours after the fish had gone to sleep. She did not want to wake up the fish. If they woke, they would exit their cocoons and Rumney would not be able to do an experiment with them. So, she did not turn the lights on; she found her way around in the dark room with a flashlight that puts out a red light. The red light did not seem to disturb the sleeping fish.

Rumney approached each container and checked that all the fish had made their cocoons. Then, she gently pushed some of the fish out of their cocoons without waking them. She took the slippery cocoon out of the container. She left the rest of the fish inside their cocoons. Next, she added isopods to all the containers and left the room.[4]

"Rumney then had to go back and check at regular times during the night to make sure all the fish continued to sleep," Grutter said. "At the end of the experiment, she returned to the room before the fish woke up to collect the parasites on the fish. She also collected the parasites in the container. She didn't sleep very much."[5]

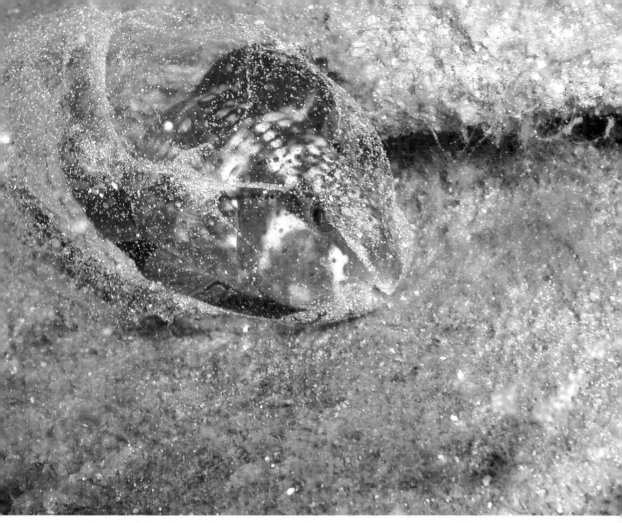

Parrotfish sleep all night inside their mucus cocoon, visible here thanks to sand sprinkled on top.

Parrotfish Don't Let the Sea Bugs Bite

Rumney counted the number of parasites she recovered from parrotfish with and without cocoons. She found that the fish that had their cocoons removed had more parasites attached to their bodies than the fish that had remained inside their cocoons. Also, the isopods Rumney recovered from the fish that had slept without cocoons had more blood inside them than the parasites from the fish inside cocoons.

The secret is out! Every night, parrotfish surround themselves with a mucus cocoon that helps ward off sea bug bites. As long as they remain in the cocoon, they are protected from blood-thirsty isopods.

3
THE SECRET OF THE HAIRY-LEGGED JUMPING SPIDER

Gil Menda studies how jumping spiders see. He places hair-sized metal electrodes into the poppy seed–sized brain of a jumping spider. Then he connects the tiny electrodes to laboratory equipment to record the electrical activity of the spider's brain.

Menda studies how jumping spiders see. He works in the lab of Professor Ron Hoy at Cornell University, New York. Menda had done this experiment many times before. He shows images on a screen to a jumping spider and records the brain activity as the spider sees the images. To know when the spider's brain responds,

Jumping spiders have excellent vision thanks to four pairs of eyes. The largest are on the middle of the front part of the body, above the iridescent fangs.

Menda connects the brain to a speaker. He hears clear "pop" sounds when the brain fires a signal.[1]

This time, however, the experiment was a little different. He was testing brain cells—neurons—deeper in the spider's brain.

Menda sat in front of a table where he had placed the spider setup, ready to begin the experiment. He moved on his chair, and it squeaked. He heard pop sounds. The brain cells were firing pulses. He moved again and heard more pop sounds coming from the speakers.

Menda was puzzled. He had not started the experiment yet! He called his colleague, Paul Shamble, who was in the next room, and told him about the squeaky chair and the popping sounds. Jumping spiders are known for their excellent vision. Nobody thought this type of spider had much of a sense of hearing, though. What was going on?[2]

Jumping Spiders Can Hear You from Across the Room

Jumping spiders are excellent daytime hunters. They do not make webs to catch prey. Instead, they stalk, chase, and jump on prey with remarkable precision. Jumping spiders use their eight eyes to judge the position and distance of insects or other spiders they want to catch. Their largest eyes, the

WHAT IS AN ELECTRODE?

An electrode is a device through which electricity travels. The tiny electrodes Gil Menda placed into the spider's brain conduct electrical signals from the brain to the laboratory equipment. The equipment transforms these signals into sounds or images that Menda can study.

pair on the front middle of their bodies, work almost as well as human eyes.[3]

All spiders can hear nearby sounds. Jumping spiders, Menda and Shamble found, can also hear sounds coming from far away.

"We started discussing the details about how spiders can only hear things close by and, to demonstrate, Paul clapped his hands close to the spider and the neuron fired, as expected," Menda said. "He then backed up a bit and clapped again, and again the neuron fired."[4]

The spider's brain continued to respond, even when the scientists clapped their hands from about 10 feet (3 meters) away. This was totally unexpected. Up until then, scientists thought that spiders were not able to hear sounds coming from more than about 2 feet (61 centimeters) away.[5] Fascinated by the discovery, Menda and Shamble decided to study it further.

A Hearing Advantage

Menda and Shamble had proof that the brain of a jumping spider could respond to faraway sounds. But, what would a spider do when it heard the sounds?

For the next experiments, the scientists placed a jumping spider on a cage that did not allow the spider to sense vibrations. The platform was in a "quiet" room. In this room the spider would only sense the sounds the scientists wanted to test and not other vibrations that might trigger a response in the spider.

Menda and Shamble set up their equipment, including a high-speed video camera to record the spider's reactions to sound. They released a spider into the cage. The spider walked about, exploring the place. The scientists played a sound. The spider stopped moving, startled by the sound. It looked around and then continued exploring. They played the sound again, and the spider stopped and scouted its surroundings with its eyes. Every time the scientists played the sound, the spider repeated the stop-and-scout behavior.[6]

Jumping spiders can hear from far away, and the sounds seem to tell them something about their environment. They stop and look around before continuing their activities. Interestingly, the scientists discovered that jumping spiders are especially sensitive to low-frequency sounds at 90 hertz.

"Why are they so sensitive to those frequencies?'" Menda asked.

After more experiments, it became clear that 90 hertz is nearly the same frequency at which parasitic wasps beat their wings. Parasitic wasps hunt jumping spiders and feed them to their young. Being able to hear parasitic wasps coming from far away gives jumping spiders a chance to escape a wasp's attack.[7]

Female jumping spiders can be as long as a jelly bean (about 0.8 inches, or 2 cm). They use their eyes to see and long hairs on their legs to hear.

Sensitive Legs

Menda and Shambles were also curious about how jumping spiders hear sounds. The spiders do not have an organ that resembles an ear or an eardrum. However, they have very hairy legs.

The scientists discovered that the hairs on the jumping spider's legs can sense sounds from far away. Jumping spiders hear with their hairy legs![8]

The secret is out! Jumping spiders can hear faraway sounds that warn them of a parasitic wasp nearby. This can help them escape the deadly predator.

4
EELS LET FOOD GET TO THEIR HEADS

Jens De Meyer, eel biologist, is dutifully cleaning the tank where he keeps European glass eels for his studies. He uses a narrow tube to remove the dirt from the tank without disturbing the eels. Most of the transparent eels, which are as long as and a bit wider than a large kitchen match (2.4 inches, or 6 cm, long and about 0.2 inches, or 5 mm, wide), swim away from the suction tube. However, one of the eels is curious.

"This eel immediately swims toward my hand when I put it inside the tank and touches me with its snout," De Meyer said. "When my colleagues and I place new rocks in the tank, this eel is the first to explore them. One day, as I was cleaning the tank, the eel swam toward the suction tube."[1]

In an instant, the eel was sucked into the tube and trapped inside it.

"For the next thirty minutes, my colleague and I tried to get the eel out. First, we tried to flush it out by running water through the tube, but this didn't work. We managed to free the eel by blowing air into the tube. This experience was probably not fun for the eel, as it was not for us. The eel never again came close to the suction tube!"[2]

Same Type of Eel, Different Head Shapes

The European eel travels great distances throughout its life cycle. Scientists think that the eels probably spawn in the Sargasso Sea, which is located in the North Atlantic Ocean. However, there is no hard evidence for this yet. Then, the Gulf Stream, an ocean current that flows east across the Atlantic Ocean, carries the larvae from North America to Europe. This amazing trip of about 4,000 miles (6,437 kilometers) lasts one to three years![3] This migration is as long as the Amazon River, the longest river on Earth.

In a nutshell, "once the larvae arrive in Europe, they transform into glass eels and migrate up the rivers," De Meyer said. "As they feed, they accumulate pigments in their bodies and become elver eels, which later become yellow eels that swim

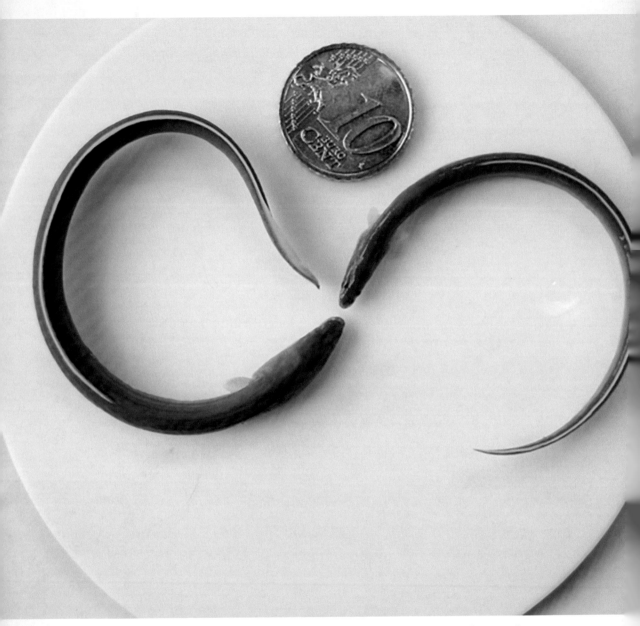

Narrow-headed and more broad-headed European eels are the same species. The eels are compared to a ten-cent euro coin, which is about the same diameter as a US nickel.

back to the Sargasso Sea, turning silver on the way." The silver eels spawn and the life cycle begins again.[4]

Interestingly, as glass eels feed and grow into yellow eels, some of them develop narrow heads while others grow broader heads. Although scientists and fishermen had known this for years, the secret of the eels with heads of different shapes remained. De Meyer and other scientists thought that the eels' diet might be linked to the shape of their head, but nobody had done experiments to prove it.

Soft Diet, Hard Diet

As De Meyer finished a series of long experiments, he had some "leftover eels" and wondered what he could do with them.

These eels are easily distinguishable by the size of their heads.

Eel growth: On the left is an eel one month after the start of the experiment. The middle eel is five months into the experiment and the one on the right is has been in for two years.

"I thought it would be a nice idea to carry out a side project with these glass eels just to find out whether we would see differences in head shape when we fed the eels different types of food," said De Meyer.[5]

The setup of the experiment was simple. De Meyer divided the eels into three aquariums. He fed soft food, such as bloodworms, to the eels in one aquarium and harder food, such as small shrimplike creatures with a hard shell, to the eels in the second aquarium. To the eels in the third group, De Meyer fed a mixture of hard and soft food.

Then he let the eels grow for several months. At different times along the way, he observed the eels with a magnifying glass, and he measured and took pictures of their heads and bodies. Three months later, he had an answer. The eels that had grown eating only soft food had a narrow head, while those that had eaten only hard food had a broader

head. Interestingly, among the eels De Meyer had fed a mixture of hard and soft foods, some had narrow heads and others had broader heads.[6]

"I was excited that in just three months, this simple experiment had revealed new important information about the eels," De Meyer said.

"My colleagues and I think that the eels in the soft-diet group developed narrow heads because they only had to suck up the bloodworms as a whole. The eels did not have to use their jaws to chew on the food," said De Meyer. "On the other hand, the eels in the hard-diet group had to work harder to eat. They sucked on their food, but also shook and bit their food harder, and spun to get the most of it. This extra work required using their jaw muscles more and this resulted in a broader head."

In the third group, which received a mixture of soft and hard food, some eels grew a narrow head while others developed a broader head. "We think that this result may show that the eels choose their food, maybe eating more of one kind than another," De Meyer said. "We still don't know what makes them choose between soft or hard food."

The secret is out! The shape of the head of the European eel depends on the type of food it eats. Eating soft foods while growing will give eels a narrow head while eating harder foods will broaden their heads.

5
THE SECRET OF THE UNDERWATER NIGHT HUMMERS

For a week in summer, Ni Feng, Andrew Bass, and their colleagues lived in a cabin near the ocean shore in Washington State. "Each morning at low tide, we'd put on boots and dirty field clothes. We'd go to the beach and lift heavy rocks to collect plainfin midshipman fish burrowed in their nests," Feng said.[1]

The field site in Washington State where Feng collects the fish is one of the feeding grounds of bald eagles. She sees the eagles scouting the grounds from high rocks, holding midshipman fish in their talons. Sometimes, she finds fish carcasses that bald eagles have discarded.

"When the tide goes out and the rocky nests are exposed, the fish are more vulnerable to predation by eagles and seagulls," Feng said.

MIDSHIPMAN FISH

What's in a Name?
Midshipman fish are widest at their flat head and can be as long as half the height of a bowling pin (about 8 inches, or 20 cm, long). "They are part of the toad-fish family and certainly have a toad-ish look!" Bass said. The fish have rows of photophores, light-producing organs, along their bodies. The lights give the fish their name because they reminded early observers of the buttons on the uniform of a midshipman, a cadet in the US Naval Academy.

"When we go out to collect the fish, the eagles are our biggest competitors!"[2]

Despite the competition, Feng caught a number of live fish. She took them to Cornell University in Ithaca, New York, where at the time she was a graduate student in Dr. Andrew Bass's laboratory. In the lab, Feng created a home for the fish.

"I set up big tanks with artificial nests made of clay disks and bricks," said Feng.

In the tanks, Feng and Bass re-created as much as possible the conditions of the fish's natural environment. Daily, they checked that the seawater in the tank remained at about 61 degrees Fahrenheit (16 degrees Celsius). They cleaned the tanks and made sure the fish ate and stayed healthy.[3] The scientists hoped that the fish would feel comfortable enough to behave the way

Ni Feng and Andrew Bass look for midshipman fish under rocks during low tide.

they do in the wild. If they did, Feng and Bass would be able to study a fascinating behavior.

Only at Night

Male plainfin midshipman fish are quite vocal when it comes to finding a mate. During the breeding season, the males migrate from deep zones in the Pacific Ocean to intertidal zones along the northwest coast of North America. The fish dig a nest in the gravel under rocks and "hum," calling females to their nests.[4]

"Males make nests close to each other and sing in choruses," said Bass. "They are competing with each other to attract females to their nests. If you are close enough to the shore, you can hear the humming sound coming from the bay."

"Although their courtship songs are simple hums, their duration is unmatched by any other fish or vertebrate species that I know," Feng said. "They can sing continuously for up to two hours and then repeat the song multiple times until a female decides to stay in the nest. They begin singing close to nightfall."

The Intertidal Zone
The intertidal zone is the seabed area exposed to the air at low tide and submerged at high tide.

The fact that male midshipman fish begin humming at nightfall and stop at sunrise intrigued Bass and Feng. Why would the fish sing nearly exclusively at night? To study this fascinating behavior, Feng brought fish to the lab and hoped they would sing in their new home.

"We were lucky that many of the fish felt comfortable in this lab environment and began singing within days of settling into their artificial homes," Feng said.

To study their songs, the scientists used a special type of microphone, called a hydrophone, that records sounds underwater.

"We placed a hydrophone in each tank and, with a computer, recorded the fish's songs continuously over days and weeks," said Feng. "This produced tremendous amounts

A male (*the larger of the two*) and a female midshipman fish are in their nest in the intertidal zone. The nest is under a rock that forms the roof of the nest.

DRUMMING MUSCLES

Midshipman fish use their swim bladder, an air-filled floating device inside their bodies, to produce humming sounds. The fish contract muscles attached to the swim bladder at a fast pace. The fast contractions make the swim bladder vibrate very quickly, like a drum. The swim bladder then causes a vibration in the surrounding water and we hear the hum.

of data. I had a team of under-graduate students who helped me tremendously with the collection and analysis of the data. We analyzed the sounds using special software."[5]

One of the first questions Feng and Bass asked was, would the fish sing if the scientists kept the lights on all the time? They didn't! The fish that were under constant light for an entire day stopped humming. On the other hand, fish that were kept on a natural cycle of light and dark hummed when the lights were off, as expected.[6] What was different in the fish's body between day and night?

The Hormone of Darkness

Feng had previously worked with hormones that affect behavior. Because midshipman fish sing only at night, she suspected that melatonin, the "hormone of darkness," might be involved in their singing.[7]

"The levels of melatonin are highest at night in almost all vertebrate species studied," Feng said.

"Most of what we know about how melatonin works in the brain comes from animals that are active during the day, but what might it be doing for an animal that is active at night?" Bass said.

The amount of melatonin increases in people's brains at night, and this helps us go to sleep. When the amount of melatonin increases at night in the brain of a bird that sings during the day, the animal doesn't sing. Was melatonin involved in the nocturnal singing of the midshipman fish?

Feng planned an experiment to "ask" this question to the singing fish in her laboratory tanks.

She divided the fish into two groups. Both groups were exposed to twenty-four hours of light. This would stop the fish from singing. The fish in one of the groups received a compound that mimicked the effects of melatonin.

THE MYSTERY OF THE HUM UNDER THE BAY

In the summer of 1984, midshipman fish raised quite a racket in San Francisco Bay. A number of fish made their nests close to a group of about 450 houseboats. When the fish sang in chorus every night, the boat owners could hardly get any sleep. It seems that the concrete or fiberglass hulls of the boats amplified the hums inside the cabins to "very irritating" levels. Some described the sound as that made by a gigantic electric shaver.

The hum started suddenly at sunset and did not stop until morning, as quickly as it had begun. Upset houseboat owners complained to the harbormaster; they thought that a malfunctioning sewage pump was causing the unbearable noise. Engineers investigated but found no equipment malfunctioning. The mystery was solved some time later when a marine biologist heard the news about the disturbing hum on San Francisco Bay. When he heard a recording of the noise, he knew at once it was the mating song of midshipman fish.[9] At least two more reports of overwhelming humming near the shore have appeared. Midshipman fish or another species of toadfish might have been involved. One was reported in Seattle in 2012 and the other in Southampton, England, in 2013.[10] What can be done about the humming? A pair of earplugs might help.

The other group did not receive any other treatments. Feng and Bass were eager to see the results.[8]

"When I walked into the fish room with constant light, I saw the fish that had received the melatonin-like compound sticking its head out of the nest and I heard the droning sound of its hum!" Feng said.

As expected, the fish that had not received the melatonin sang very little compared to those that had received melatonin.

"It's a great feeling when experiments work and your predictions turn out to be true," Feng said.

The secret of the night hummers is out! Melatonin works in opposite ways in midshipman fish and in birds. At night, the hormone turns on the hum in the fish and turns off singing in birds.

HANDS-ON ACTIVITY: ON TIME

Living organisms do certain activities on cycles or repeated sequences. For instance, people go through daily periods of sleep followed by periods of being awake. Your body temperature changes throughout the day, and some hormones in your body do, too, in a cyclic manner. The singing fish sings at night and stays quiet during the day, and it repeats the cycle every day for part of the year. Birds follow the opposite cycle; they sing during the day and sleep at night. This twenty-four-hour cycle of activity is called the circadian rhythm.

Living organisms have an internal clock for keeping time to carry out their circadian rhythms. This internal clock also helps us estimate time. In this activity you will test a friend's and your internal stopwatch.

What you need:
- ★ stopwatch
- ★ paper and pencil

What to do:
1. Ask a friend to help you do the experiment.
2. Instruct your friend to begin counting seconds aloud when you start the stopwatch and to stop counting when you stop the stopwatch.
3. Before you start the stopwatch, choose, in any order, the time you will test: 5, 10, 15, 30, or 60 seconds. Don't tell your friend which one you chose.

4. Start the stopwatch and stop when you reach the selected time.
5. Write down the time your friend counted in a copy of the table below. (Don't show your friend the table until you have finished testing his/her internal clock.)
6. Repeat steps 4 and 5 for the rest of the times.
7. Repeat the experiment, this time with you counting and your friend keeping time.

Stopwatch time (seconds)	Your friend's time (seconds)	Your time (seconds)
5		
10		
15		
30		
60		

Discuss:
1. Were your friend's and your internal clocks on time with the stopwatch?
2. If not, how can you better synchronize your internal clock with the stopwatch?

★ CHAPTER NOTES ★

Chapter 1: The Shocking Secret of the Electric Eel

1. Laurence Denis, "Electric Eels Leap from Water in Shock Video. Defensive Electrocution Added to Annals of Electric Fish Behaviour," *Nature*, doi:10.1038/nature.2016.20038, June 6, 2016.

2. Kenneth Catania, "Leaping Eels Electrify Threats, Supporting Humboldt's Account of a Battle with Horses," *Proceedings of the National Academy of Sciences*, vol. 113, 2016, p. 6979.

3. Ibid.

4. Kenneth Catania, "The Shocking Predatory Strike of the Electric Eel," *Science*, vol. 346, 2014, p. 1231.

5. Ibid.

6. Ibid.

7. Catania, 2016.

Chapter 2: Parrotfish Don't Let the Sea Bugs Bite

1. Dr. Alexandra Grutter, Skype interview with author, October 23, 2016.

2. Alexandra S. Grutter, Jennifer G. Rumney, Tane Sinclair-Taylor, Peter Waldie, and Craig E. Franklin, "Fish Mucous Cocoons: The 'Mosquito Nets' of the Sea," *Biology Letters*, vol. 7, 2011, p. 292.

3. Dr. Grutter interview.

4. Grutter, et al.

5. Dr. Grutter interview.

Chapter 3: The Secret of the Hairy-Legged Jumping Spider

1. Krishna Ramanujan, "Jumping Spiders Can Hear at a Distance, New Study Proves," *Cornell Chronicle*, October 13, 2016, http://news.cornell.edu/stories/2016/10/jumping-spiders-can-hear-distance-new-study-proves.

2. Phys.org, "That Jumping Spider Can hear You from Across the Room," October 13, 2016, https://phys.org/news/2016-10-spider -room.html.

3. Ramanujan.

4. Phys.org.

5. Paul S. Shamble, Eyal I. Nitzany, Katherine Walden, Tsevi Beatus, Damian O. Elias, Itai Cohen, Ronald N. Miles, and Ronald R. Hoy, "Airborne Acoustic Perception by a Jumping Spider," *Current Biology*, vol. 26, 2016, p. 2913.

6. Ibid.

7. Ibid.

8. Ibid.

Chapter 4: Eels Let Food Get to Their Heads

1. Dr. Jens De Meyer, email interview with author, October 11, 2016.

2. Ibid.

3. Jens De Meyer, Joachim Christiaens, and Dominique Adriaens, "Diet-induced Phenotypic Plasticity in European Eel (*Anguilla anguilla*)," *Journal of Experimental Biology*, vol. 219, 2016, p. 354.

4. Dr. De Meyer interview.

5. Ibid.

6. De Meyer, et al.

Chapter 5: The Secret of the Underwater Night Hummers

1. Dr. Ni Feng, email interview with author, February 18, 2017.

2. Ibid.

3. Dr. Andrew Bass, Skype interview with author, February 16, 2017.

4. Ni Y. Feng, Andrew H. Bass, "'Singing' Fish Rely on Circadian Rhythm and Melatonin for the Timing of Nocturnal Courtship Vocalization," *Current Biology*, vol. 26, 2016, p. 2681.

5. Dr. Feng interview.

6. Feng and Bass.

7. Dr. Feng interview.

8. Feng and Bass.

9. Jay Stuller, "Things That Go Hum in the Night," *Audubon*, vol. 88, 1986, p. 120.

10. Rick Spilman, "The Hum Heard Round the World—From Sausalito to Seattle to Southhampton, Mating Midshipmen Fish Keeping the Neighbors Awake," *The Old Salt Blog*, October 25, 2013, http://www.oldsaltblog.com/2013/10/the-hum-heard-round -the-world-from-sausalito-to-seattle-to-south-hampton-mating -midshipmen-fish-keeping-the-neighbors-awake.

★ GLOSSARY ★

cocoon ★ A protective enclosed covering.

electrocyte ★ A modified muscle cell that generates electricity.

hydrophone ★ A microphone that works underwater.

insulation ★ A material that prevents the passage of electricity, heat, or sound.

intertidal zone ★ The area of coastline between the low-tide and high-tide marks.

isopod ★ Small hard-shelled organism similar to lice that is a parasite to other creatures.

larvae ★ The young of invertebrate animals.

melatonin ★ A hormone produced at night.

mucus ★ A slimy substance.

neuron ★ A type of cell in the brain and the nervous system.

photophore ★ An organ that gives out light.

predator ★ An animal that hunts others animals for food.

spawn ★ To produce offspring.

★ FURTHER READING ★

Books

Archer, Claire. *Jumping Spiders*. North Mankato, MN: Capstone Classroom, 2016.

Hamilton, S. L. *Eels*. Minneapolis MN: ABDO & Daughters, 2014.

Montgomery, Sy. *Amazon Adventure: How Tiny Fish Are Saving the World's Largest Rainforest*. New York, NY: HMH Books for Young Readers, 2017.

Wittlinger, Ellen. *Parrotfish*. New York, NY: Simon & Schuster Books for Young Readers, 2015.

Websites

National Geographic
animals.nationalgeographic.com/animals/fish/electric-eel
Learn more about the electric eel.

Science News
youtube.com/watch?v=nNB-hoKwa0A
Hear the midshipman's "song."

★ INDEX ★

B
Bass, Andrew, 31, 32–39

C
Catania, Kenneth, 5–7, 9–10
circadian rhythm activity, 40–41
cleaner fish, 13

D
De Meyer, Jens, 24–30

E
electric eel, 4, 5–10
   electric pulses, 7–10
   leap-and-shock attack, 4, 5–7,
      9–10
electrocytes, 7
electrodes, 17, 19
European eel, 4, 24–30
   head size, 27–30

F
Feng, Ni, 31–39

G
gnathiid isopod, 12–13, 14–16
Grutter, Alexandra, 11–12, 13, 14

H
Humboldt, Alexander von, 6, 10

I
intertidal zones, 33, 34

J
jumping spider, 4, 17–23
   ability to hear, 4, 19, 20–21, 23

M
melatonin, 36–39
Menda, Gil, 17–19, 20–21, 23

midshipman fish, 31–39
   singing, 33–39
   swim bladder, 36

N
neurons, 18

P
parasitic wasps, 21, 23
parrotfish, 4, 11–16
   mucus cocoon, 4, 11–12, 13–16
photophores, 32

R
Rumney, Jennifer, 11, 12, 13, 14–15

S
Shamble, Paul, 19, 20–21, 23
symbiosis, 13